P9-EAJ-153

SCIENCE FAIR PROJECTS

Ecosystems

Natalie Rompella

Heinemann Library
Chicago, Illinois

Customer Service 888-454-2279
Visit our website at www.heinemannlibrary.com

Produced for Heinemann Library by White-Thomson Publishing Ltd.
Page layout by Tim Mayer and Alison Walper
Edited by Brian Fitzgerald
Photo research by Amy Sparks
Illustrations by Cavedweller Studio
Printed and bound in China by Leo Paper Group
12 11 10 09 08
10 9 8 7 6 5 4 3 2 1

Library of Congress Cataloging-in-Publication Data
Rompella, Natalie.
   Ecosystems / Natalie Rompella. — 1st ed.
      p. cm. — (Science fair projects)
   Includes bibliographical references and index.
   ISBN 978-1-4034-7915-0 (hc)
   1. Ecology—Experiments—Juvenile literature. 2. Ecology
projects—Juvenile literature. I. Title.
   QH541.24.R66 2007
   577—dc22
                                         2006039543

Acknowledgments
The author and publishers are grateful to the following for permission to reproduce copyright
material: Alamy/Aliki Sapountzi/aliki image library, **p. 16**; iStockphoto.com, **title page, pp. 9
(inset), 36, 6** (Peter Van Wagner), **6 (inset)** (Claire Desjardins), **8** (Lidian Neeleman), **9** (Carmen
Martãnez), **11** (Midwest Wilderness), **20** (Terry Healy), **24** (Joop Snijder), **26** (Thorsten Golditz),
28 (David Raboin), **32** (Greg Okimi), **35** (Steven Allan); Masterfile/Andrew Douglas, **p. 4**; NHPA,
pp. 12 (Jari Peltomaki), **40** (Paal Hermansen); Photolibrary/Kidd Geoff, **p. 9**.

Cover photograph reproduced with permission of Cathy Kelfer/istockphoto.com

The publishers would like to thank Sue Glass for her assistance in the preparation of this book.

Every effort has been made to contact copyright holders of any material reproduced
in this book. Any omissions will be rectified in subsequent printings if notice is given
to the publisher.

Disclaimer
All the Internet addresses (URLs) given in this book were valid at the time of going to press.
However, due to the dynamic nature of the Internet, some addresses may have changed, or
sites may have changed or ceased to exist since publication. While the author and publisher
regret any inconvenience this may cause readers, no responsibility for any such changes can be
accepted by either the author or the publisher.

 Some words are shown in bold, **like this.** You can
find the definitions for these words in the glossary.

Contents

Science fair Basics

Starting a science fair project can be an exciting challenge. You can test a **scientific theory** by developing an appropriate scientific question. Then you can search, using the thoughtful steps of a well-planned experiment, for the answer to that question. It's like a treasure hunt of the mind.

In a way, your mission is to better understand how your world and the things in it work. You may be rewarded with a good grade or an award for your scientific hard work. But no matter what scores your project receives, you'll be a winner. That's because you will know a little bit more about your subject than you did before you started.

There are many different ecosystems in action everywhere, and each is unique. An **ecosystem** is all the living and nonliving things interacting with one another in a certain area. In this book, you'll discover how factors such as overcrowding, water, and decomposers affect ecosystems.

Do Your Research

Is there something about ecosystems you've always wondered about? Something you don't quite understand but would like to? Then do a little research about the subject. Go to the library and check out books about the subject that interests you.

Use your favorite Internet search engine to find reliable online sources. Museums, universities, scientific journals, newspapers, and magazines are among the best sources for accurate research. Each experiment in this book lists some suggestions for further research.

The Experiments

Project Information

The beginning of each experiment contains a box like this.

Possible Question:

This question is a suggested starting point for your experiment. You will need to adapt the question to reflect your own interests.

Materials Needed:

Make sure you can easily get all of the materials listed and gather them before beginning work.

Possible Hypothesis:

Don't worry if your hypothesis doesn't match the one listed here; this is only a suggestion.

Approximate Cost of Materials:

Discuss this with your parents before beginning work.

Level of Difficulty:

There are three levels of experiments in this book: Easy, Intermediate, and Advanced. The level of difficulty is based on how long the experiment takes and how complicated it is.

When doing research, you need to make sure your sources are reliable. Ask yourself the following questions about sources, especially those you find online.

1) How old is the source? Is it possible that the information is outdated?

2) Who wrote the source? Is there an identifiable author, and is the author qualified to write about the topic?

3) What is the purpose of the source? The website of a potato chip company is probably not the best place to look for information on healthful diets.

4) Is the information well documented? Can you tell where the author got his or her information?

Some websites allow you to "chat" online with experts. Make sure you discuss this with your parent or teacher before participating. Never give out private information, including your address or phone number, online.

Continued ⊙

Both frozen polar areas and grassy swamps (inset) are examples of ecosystems.

Once you know a bit more about the subject you want to explore, you'll be ready to ask a science project question and form an intelligent **hypothesis.** A hypothesis is an educated guess about what the results of your experiment will be. Finally, you'll be ready to begin your science fair exploration!

What is an Experiment?

When you say you're going to "experiment," you may just mean that you're going to try something out. When a scientist uses that word, though, he or she means something else. In a proper experiment, you have **variables** and a **control.** A variable is something that changes. The independent variable is the thing you purposely change as part of the experiment. The dependent variable is the change that happens in response to the thing you do. The controlled variables, or control group, are the things you do not change so that you have something to compare your outcomes with. Here's an example: You want to test whether fertilizer really helps grass grow. You add fertilizer to three cups of grass seed (Group A). You do not add fertilizer to three other cups of grass seed (Group B). The fertilizer is the independent variable. The growth rate of the grass is the dependent variable. Group B is a control group. Using a large sample of cups for both the variable and control groups will increase the accuracy of the results of your experiment.

Some of the projects in this book are not proper experiments. They are projects designed to help you learn about a subject. You need to check with your teacher about whether these projects are appropriate for your science fair. Before beginning a project, make sure you know the rules about what kinds of projects and materials are allowed.

Your Hypothesis

Once you've decided what question you're going to try to answer, you'll want to make a scientific **prediction** of what you'll discover through your science project. For example, if you wonder what effect acid rain has on plant growth, your question might be, "Does acid affect plant growth?"

Remember, your hypothesis states the results you expect from your experiment. So your hypothesis in response to the above question might be, "The amount of acid will affect plant growth." Your research question also offers a good way to find out whether you can actually complete the steps needed for a successful project. If your question is, "What one factor changes an ecosystem?", it will be impossible to test your hypothesis, no matter how you express it. So, be sure the evidence to support your hypothesis is actually within reach.

Research Journal

It is very important to keep careful notes about your project. From start to finish, make entries in your research journal so you won't have to rely on memory when it is time to create your display. What time did you start your experiment? How long did you work on it each day? What were the variables, or things that changed, about your experimental setting? How did they change and why? What things did you overlook in planning your project? How did you solve the problems, once you discovered them?

These are the kinds of questions you'll answer in your research journal. No detail is too small when it comes to scientific research. On pages 44–46 of this book, you'll find some tips on writing your report and preparing a winning display. Use these and the tips in each project as guides, but don't be afraid to get creative. Make your display, and your project, your own.

My Personal Ecosystem

Did you know that there are many different ecosystems near your home or school? An ecosystem doesn't have to be huge. It could be as small as your backyard—or even smaller, such as the area around a tree. In this experiment, you will choose one ecosystem to observe over time.

Do Your Research

For this project, you will note changes to **biotic** factors. These are living things, such as plants and animals. You may also notice changes to **abiotic** factors—nonliving things, such as rocks and water. Research the plants, trees, and animals that live in the ecosystem you are studying. Don't forget to learn about the insects and other small creatures that also play an important role in any ecosystem. Then you'll be ready to begin this project or come up with your own.

Here are some books and websites you could start with in your research:

» Davis, Barbara. *Ecosystems and Biomes*. Milwaukee: Gareth Stevens, 2007.
» Real Trees 4 Kids: What's the System?
http://www.realtrees4kids.org/ninetwelve/system.htm
» What Tree Is It? http://www.oplin.org/tree

Project Information

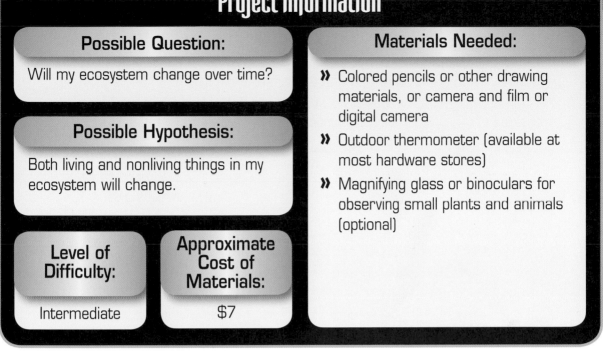

Possible Question:

Will my ecosystem change over time?

Possible Hypothesis:

Both living and nonliving things in my ecosystem will change.

Level of Difficulty:

Intermediate

Approximate Cost of Materials:

$7

Materials Needed:

» Colored pencils or other drawing materials, or camera and film or digital camera

» Outdoor thermometer (available at most hardware stores)

» Magnifying glass or binoculars for observing small plants and animals (optional)

Steps to Success:

1. Choose an area that you will be able to observe frequently, such as your backyard or an area around your school. It should be a place with at least one tree and some other plants.

Observing ants and other small creatures can help you better understand an ecosystem.

Continued ⊖

2. Write the date and time in your research journal. Then make a detailed drawing or take a picture showing the different plants and animals you see. Label each photo or drawing. Be sure to look closely at the ground for insects and signs of animals, such as droppings, chewed leaves or nuts, burrows, even footprints. Look back at your sources or in field guides to help identify any unknown plants or creatures.

Step 2

September 10
Time: 9:00 A.M.

Temperature: 67° F (19° C).
Weather: Sunny

Notes:
• The grass and leaves on the oak tree are damp from the rain last night.
• I saw two squirrels running up and down the tree. They carried leaves and acorns.
• A bee buzzed around the tree.
• A caterpillar crawled on the small rock next to the tree.

Photo of squirrel taken September 10

3. Choose specific factors to look for each day, such as the number of leaves on the ground or how many ants you count. Note this **data** in your research journal. Also record the temperature and weather conditions—is it rainy, sunny, or cloudy?

4. The next day, observe your ecosystem again, looking for the same factors you observed the day before.

5. Continue to observe your ecosystem and note any changes for two weeks.

Result Summary:

» What did you observe about the plants in your ecosystem?

» What did you observe about the animals in your ecosystem?

» Did changes in the weather conditions seem to have an effect on your ecosystem?

» Did any of the abiotic (nonliving) factors change, such as the light levels or temperature?

Added Activities to Give Your Project Extra Punch:

» Compare two different ecosystems, such as one that gets a lot of sunlight with one that gets less, to see whether the biotic (living) factors differ.

» Extend the project by observing the same ecosystem at different times of the year, such as in spring and in winter, and comparing the different factors.

Display Extras:

» Display your ecosystem drawings or photos.

» Present some of the factors you observed, such as temperature, in a table or graph.

Binoculars allow you to closely observe birds and other biotic factors in the treetops.

What Was for Lunch?

Every ecosystem has a **food chain**—a process in which food energy is transferred from small organisms to larger ones. Plants are **producers.** They use the energy they receive from sunlight to create their own food. Animals that are **herbivores** eat the plants. Other animals, **carnivores,** eat those animals. Other carnivores eat those animals, and so on up the chain. In this project, you will see whether you can piece together the food chain by examining what an owl ate.

Do Your Research

Owls are carnivores. When an owl catches its prey, it eats the entire creature, including the bones and fur. Then the owl **regurgitates** the parts of the prey its body doesn't need, in the form of a pellet. For this project, you will need to buy owl pellets from a special company. Most companies heat-sterilize the pellets, but you should still wear rubber or latex gloves and wash your hands and your work surface after handling the pellet. If you are allergic to fur, this project may not be safe for you.

Before you get started, learn about the food chain and food webs. You should also do some research on owls, including where they live and what animals they prey upon. Because you will be reconstructing an animal skeleton, you will need bone charts for owls' most common prey. Then you will be ready to begin the project or come up with a similar one.

Project Information

Possible Question:

How can I study what an owl eats?

Possible Hypothesis:

I will be able to discover what an owl eats by studying its pellets.

Level of Difficulty:

Advanced

Approximate Cost of Materials:

$20

Materials Needed:

» Newspaper
» Bone identification charts

Materials Needed (cont.):

» Plastic gloves (you may be able to get some from a local deli or your doctor's office)
» Two or three owl pellets (available from many online sources; search by typing "owl pellet" into a trusted search engine)
» Toothpicks
» Pieces of cardboard, each approximately 7 inches by 10 inches (18 centimeters by 25 centimeters), one for each pellet
» Fine-point marker
» Glue
» Gallon-size resealable plastic bags, one for each pellet

Here are some books and websites you could start with in your research:

» Kalman, Bobbie D. *Food Chains and You.* New York: Crabtree, 2005.
» Spilsbury, Richard and Louise. *Food Chains and Webs: From Producers to Decomposers.* Chicago: Heinemann, 2004.
» KidWings: Virtual Owl Pellet Dissection
http://www.kidwings.com/owlpellets
» Carolina Biological: The Secret Lives of Owls: Owl Pellets
http://www.carolina.com/owls/guide/pellets.asp
Follow the links at the bottom of the page to bone identification charts for each of the owl's prey.

Continued ⊕

1. Cover your work area with newspaper. Lay the bone identification charts close by so you can refer to them as you work. Put on the gloves before you open the pellet.

2. Remove the pellet from its wrapper. Use both hands to carefully pull the pellet into two pieces. Some bones might be exposed. Use a toothpick to separate the bones from any fur or feathers. Clean the bones with the toothpick and your hands. Set the bones to the side.

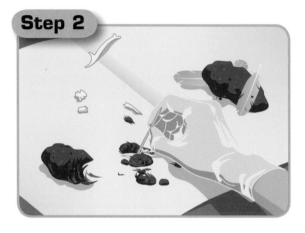

Step 2

3. Continue to pull the ball into smaller chunks and to separate the bones. After you have investigated the entire pellet, use the bone identification charts to try to determine what creature the owl ate and to identify each bone. Jawbones and skulls are usually the best clues for identifying what animal the owl ate.

4. Organize the bones on the cardboard. Use the bone identification charts to try to reconstruct the animal's skeleton. Most bones will probably be from a single animal, but you may find bones from more than one creature in a single pellet.

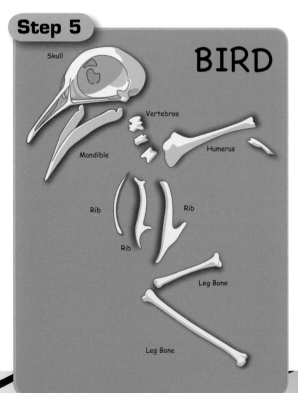

Step 5

BIRD

Skull

Vertebrae

Mandible

Humerus

Rib

Rib

Rib

Leg Bone

Leg Bone

5. Write the name of the prey on the cardboard. Glue the bones to the cardboard, labeling any ones you can identify.

6. When the glue is dry, carefully place the cardboard in the plastic bag. Be sure to seal the bag.

7. Repeat steps 2–6 with the other pellets.

8. When you are finished, roll the pellet remains in newspaper and throw them away. Also throw away your gloves, and then wash your hands thoroughly.

Result Summary:

» What animals' remains did you find in your pellets?
» What were some of the differences in what you found in each pellet?

Added Activities to Give Your Project Extra Punch:

» Order different owl species' pellets from another company, which would have collected the pellets from different locations. Compare what those owls ate with what you found in the original pellets.

» Research the eating habits of the animal whose bones you found in the owl pellet. Use this information to construct the food chain for the ecosystem in which the owl lives.

» Research and report on the special adaptations, such as night vision and excellent hearing, that make owls such effective hunters.

Display Extras:

» Display the cardboard with the animal bones glued to it.
» Include pictures of the creatures you found in the pellets in their natural habitats.
» Attach photos of an owl swooping down to attack its prey.
» Include the bone identification charts.

I'm Crowded!

Have you ever seen a photo of clowns stuffed into a tiny car? It doesn't look as if it would be very comfortable. We know that people and animals need space to flourish, but do plants? In this experiment, you'll find out by planting many seeds in a small space.

Do Your Research

Before you get started, learn about the seeds and plants you will be using. What should they look like as they grow? How fast should they grow? You should also do some research on overcrowding of plants and **carrying capacity**—the maximum number of a species that an area can support. Once you've done your research, you may decide to vary this project or follow the directions listed here.

Here are some books and websites you could start with in your research:

» Kudlinski, Kathleen V. *How Plants Survive*. Philadelphia: Chelsea Clubhouse, 2003.

» Why Plants Need Space Too: http://www.units.muohio.edu/dragonfly/itc/one.html

» The Great Plant Escape: In Search of Green Life
http://www.urbanext.uiuc.edu/gpe/case1/c1facts3a.html

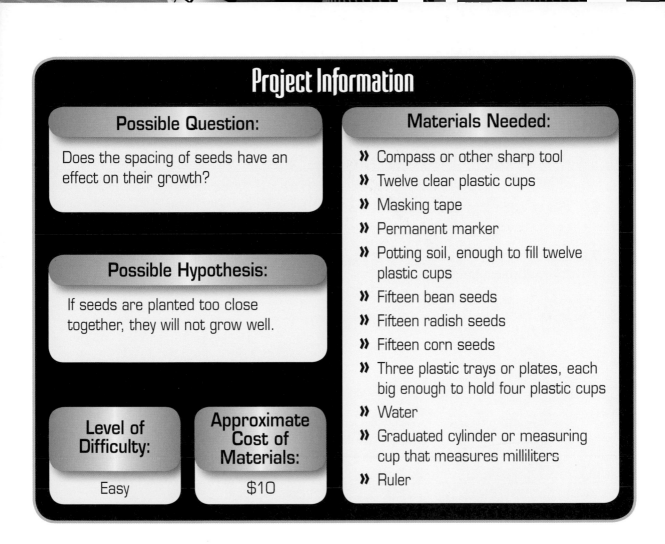

Project Information

Possible Question:

Does the spacing of seeds have an effect on their growth?

Possible Hypothesis:

If seeds are planted too close together, they will not grow well.

Level of Difficulty:

Easy

Approximate Cost of Materials:

$10

Materials Needed:

» Compass or other sharp tool
» Twelve clear plastic cups
» Masking tape
» Permanent marker
» Potting soil, enough to fill twelve plastic cups
» Fifteen bean seeds
» Fifteen radish seeds
» Fifteen corn seeds
» Three plastic trays or plates, each big enough to hold four plastic cups
» Water
» Graduated cylinder or measuring cup that measures milliliters
» Ruler

Steps to Success:

1. Use the compass to carefully poke a few holes in the bottom of each plastic cup.

2. Prepare three separate cups for each type of seed. Label each cup with the name of the seed and number them 1, 2, and 3. Label the three remaining cups All Seeds and number them 1, 2, and 3.

3. Fill each cup with potting soil to within ½ inch (1.25 centimeters) of the top.

Continued →

4. Poke your finger about ½ inch (1.25 centimeters) into the center of the soil. For the individual seed cups, drop one seed into the hole and cover with soil. For each of the All Seeds cups, place four of each seed in the hole and cover with soil.

5. Place the four cups labeled 1 on one of the trays. Place the cups labeled 2 and 3 on the other two trays. Put the trays in an area that gets a lot of sunlight. Be sure to wash your hands after touching the soil.

6. Water each cup just enough to moisten the soil, about 60 milliliters. Leave any water that drains through on the tray.

7. Observe the cups daily. If the soil is dry to the touch, add about 30 milliliters of water to each cup.

Step 8

8. Record the day that each seed begins to sprout, or **germinate.** Use the individual plant cups as a guide to which seeds are germinating in the All Seeds cup. Once the plants begin to grow, measure the height of each plant. Also note how many leaves it grows and record any changes in the plant's appearance.

9. Continue to record the growth of the seeds for two weeks. Compare the growth of the individual seeds with the growth of the seeds in the All Seeds cups.

Result Summary:

» Which plant in the individual cups germinated first?

» Which plant in the individual cups grew the tallest?

» Did all the seeds in each of the All Seeds cups germinate?

» Which plant in the All Seeds cups germinated first?

» Which plant in the All Seeds cups grew the tallest?

» Did any of the seeds in the All Seeds cups have unexpected or unusual growth patterns?

» Did the number of seeds affect the growth of the plants?

Added Activities to Give Your Project Extra Punch:

» Show the average height of the different plant types in the All Seeds cup on your results table.

» Use different types of seeds, such as grass or flowers, and compare the results with those in the original project.

» Test how many seeds are too many. In different cups, plant varying numbers of the same kind of seed in a single hole in the soil. Compare the plant growth in all of the cups.

» Plant sunflower seeds in the cup with the other seeds. Sunflowers are **allelopathic,** which means they release a chemical that prevents other plants from growing near them. Research other allelopathic plants as well.

Display Extras:

» Take a picture of the plants every other day. Include the photos on your board.

» Compare the growth of the single plants with the growth of the plants in the All Seeds cup in both graph and table forms.

Trapped in a Greenhouse

The **atmosphere,** the layer of gases surrounding Earth, is important to life on our planet. It keeps moisture and heat "trapped" near the surface of Earth. This is called the natural **greenhouse effect.** Plants are often grown in greenhouses (above), where sunlight can enter but heat can't easily escape. To see greenhouses in action, you'll compare the growth of plants in sealed containers with that of plants grown in open containers.

Do Your Research

Before you start, research the greenhouse effect, how it heats Earth, and how it enables plants to grow. Also research the atmosphere and its role in the **water cycle,** the process in which Earth's water is constantly recycled. In this project, you'll observe the water cycle on a small scale in the sealed plastic bag. Once you've done your research, you'll be ready for this project or a similar one of your own.

Here are some books and websites you could start with in your research:

» Cosgrove, Brian. *Eyewitness: Weather*. New York: Dorling Kindersley, 2004.

» Gallant, Roy A. *Atmosphere: Sea of Air*. New York: Benchmark, 2003.

» The Water Cycle: http://www.kidzone.ws/water/

» EPA Climate Change Kids Site: Greenhouse Effect
http://epa.gov/climatechange/kids/greenhouse.html

Project Information

Possible Question:

Will seeds planted in a closed container grow differently from those planted in an open container?

Possible Hypothesis:

Plants in a sealed container will grow faster than plants in an open container.

Level of Difficulty:

Easy

Approximate Cost of Materials:

$10

Materials Needed:

» Compass or other sharp tool
» Six clear plastic cups
» Masking tape
» Permanent marker
» Potting soil, enough to fill six plastic cups
» Six bean seeds (dried beans sold in bags at the grocery store will work)
» Graduated cylinder or measuring cup that measures milliliters
» Water
» Three gallon-size resealable plastic freezer bags
» Two identical thermometers
» Ruler

Steps to Success:

1. Use the compass to carefully poke a few holes in the bottom of each plastic cup.

2. Label three plastic cups Open and number them 1, 2, and 3. Label the other three cups Sealed and number them 1, 2, and 3.

3. Fill all six plastic cups with soil to within ½ inch (1.25 centimeters) of the top.

4. Poke your finger about ½ inch (1.25 centimeters) into the center of the soil in each cup. Place one bean seed in each hole and cover with soil.

Continued ⟶

5. Water each cup with an equal amount of water, about 60 milliliters.

6. Put one of the cups labeled Sealed in each of the plastic bags. Place a thermometer in one of the bags. Blow in the bags to puff them out with air, and then seal the bags.

7. Place all the cups by a window where they will receive an equal amount of sunlight. Place one thermometer near the Open cups. Be sure to keep the bags out of the reach of small children and pets.

Step 7

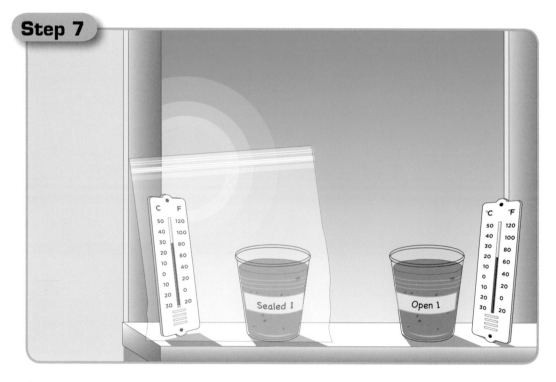

8. Observe the cups daily. Record the day that each seed germinates. Also record the temperature in the sealed bag and the room temperature near the open containers. Note how the soil in each cup looks each day.

9. Once the plants begin to grow, measure them daily; record the growth in your research journal. Measure the growth of the plants in the sealed containers from the outside of the bag. **Do not open the bags.**

10. Continue to observe plant growth for ten days. Compare the growth of the plants in the open and sealed cups.

Result Summary:

» Did the plants in the open or sealed containers germinate first?

» Did the plants in the open or sealed containers grow taller?

» What did the soil in the open containers look like at the end of the experiment?

» What did the soil in the sealed containers look like at the end of the experiment?

Added Activities to Give Your Project Extra Punch:

» Repeat the experiment with different types of seeds.

» Put all the seeds in sealed bags but vary the amount of water in each. Be sure to also record the temperature in each.

Display Extras:

» Include a photo or an illustration of the plants. Be sure the labels are visible.

» Show the growth results in both table and graph forms.

» Include the grown bean plants as part of your display.

» Create a diagram showing how a greenhouse keeps the heat in.

Invaders!

You've probably seen weeds or other unwanted plants near your home or school. Many are plants that were brought from another area. Without natural enemies, these plants took over the space of the native plants. These intruders are called **invasives.** In this project, you will locate invasive plants around your city or town and see what effect they have on other plants.

Do Your Research

It is best to do this project in spring, when non-native invasive plants are most plentiful. *Non-native* refers to plants that are not originally from the area. Not all non-native plants are invasive. Some common invasive plants in the United States are dandelions (above) and purple loosestrife.

Before you get started, research the plants in your area. It is a good idea to speak with a plant expert at your local gardening store or greenhouse. He or she can help you learn about which plants are invasive and how they affect native plant life. Once you know what to look for, you can begin this project or come up with your own.

Project Information

Possible Question:

What invasive plants are found in my town, and how do they affect the surrounding plants?

Materials Needed:

» Camera and film or digital camera, or drawing supplies

Possible Hypothesis:

Non-native invasive plants make it difficult for native species to grow.

Level of Difficulty:

Advanced

Approximate Cost of Materials:

$10

Here are some books and websites you could start with in your research:

» May, Suellen. *Invasive Terrestrial Plants*. New York: Chelsea House, 2006.

» Souza, D. M. *Plant Invaders*. Danbury, Conn.: Watts Library, 2004.

» Science News for Kids: Alien Invasions
http://www.sciencenewsforkids.org/articles/20040512/Feature1.asp

» The United States National Arboretum: Invasive Plants
http://www.usna.usda.gov/Gardens/invasives.html

» National Park Service: Invasive Species: A Knowledge Center
http://www2.nature.nps.gov/views/KCs/Invasives/Invasives_Index.htm

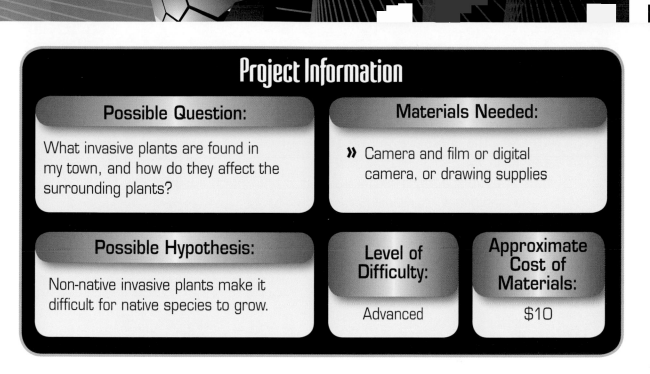

Japanese knotweed is native to Asia but is found as an invasive species throughout the United States.

Continued

Steps to Success:

1. Research what plants are invasive to your area. The books and websites listed in Do Your Research will help you locate invasive species in your area. A gardening pro at your local garden or home center might also be a good resource. Learn what the invasive species look like and where they are most likely to be found—such as near water, where the soil is dry, or in areas that get a lot of sunlight.

2. Walk or bike around your area to locate the invasive plants.

3. Take photos or draw pictures of the plants. After you take a picture, write the number of the photo, the plant name, and the area in which you found the plant in your research journal.

4. Also note the effect the invasives seem to have on surrounding plants, including grass. For example, how much of the area do the invasive plants cover, and do they appear to have caused the surrounding grass to die? Find areas that don't include the invasive plant; compare the condition of the plants and grass there with those in areas where the invasive is present.

Purple loosestrife is an invasive plant that thrives in wet areas.

Step 3

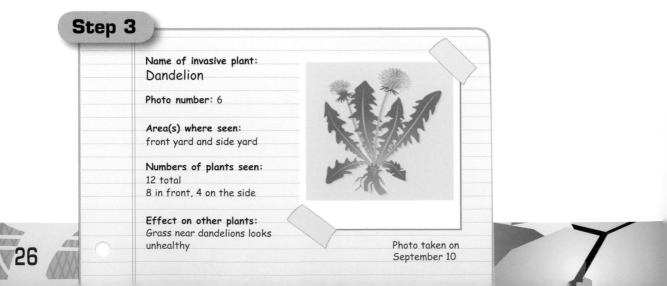

Name of invasive plant:
Dandelion

Photo number: 6

Area(s) where seen:
front yard and side yard

Numbers of plants seen:
12 total
8 in front, 4 on the side

Effect on other plants:
Grass near dandelions looks
unhealthy

Photo taken on
September 10

Result Summary:

» How many different invasive plants did you find in your area?

» Which invasive plant did you see in the most places?

» Where did you find most invasive plants (near water, in sunny areas, in shady areas)?

» What effect did the invasive plants seem to have on the native plants?

Added Activities to Give Your Project Extra Punch:

» Observe invasive plants over a longer time period, using a **quadrat survey.** In this type of survey, you measure two equal-size sample sections (each 1 square yard, for example) of a larger area and compare your observations in each section.

» Research common invasive plants, such as dandelions. Find out where they originated and when they were introduced to your part of the country.

» Take the project a step further by researching animal species that are invasive in your area.

Display Extras:

» Include your photos or drawings of the invasive plants.

» Attach a map of the area you observed and note the spots where you found invasive plants.

» If possible, collect samples of the invasive species and display them.

Water Cleaned with Dirt?

Did you know that Earth is a natural filter? It might be hard to believe, but soil and rocks are natural cleaners. They help life in an ecosystem by filtering the water used by humans, animals, and plants. In this experiment, you will create your own filters and compare how well they clean dirty water.

Do Your Research

Before you get started, research how water is filtered through layers of sediment and ends up as **groundwater.** Groundwater is water found in underground streams between rocks and soil. You should also learn about how wetlands and other areas act as purifiers for our water. Then you'll be ready to tackle this project, or you can change the setup to make it your own.

Here are some books and websites you could start with in your research:

» Ballard, Carol. *How We Use Water*. Chicago: Raintree, 2005.

» Gallant, Roy A. *Water: Our Precious Resource*. New York: Benchmark, 2003.

» Earth's Water: Ground Water: http://ga.water.usgs.gov/edu/earthgw.html

» Teacher's Domain: Earth Water Filter: http://www.teachersdomain.org/resources/ess05/sci/ess/earthsys/waterfilter

» Importance of Wetlands
http://www.mbgnet.net/fresh/wetlands/index.htm

Project Information

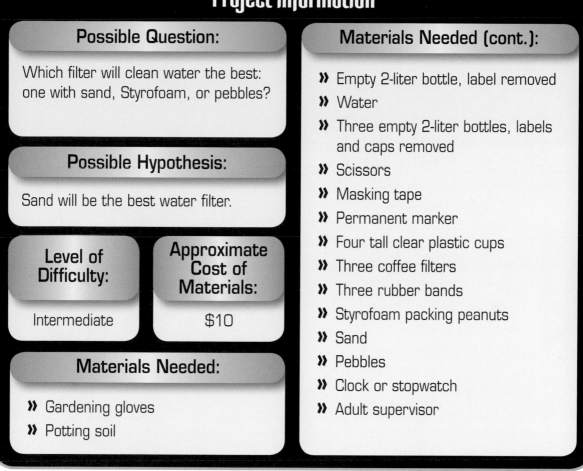

Possible Question:

Which filter will clean water the best: one with sand, Styrofoam, or pebbles?

Possible Hypothesis:

Sand will be the best water filter.

Level of Difficulty:

Intermediate

Approximate Cost of Materials:

$10

Materials Needed:

» Gardening gloves
» Potting soil

Materials Needed (cont.):

» Empty 2-liter bottle, label removed
» Water
» Three empty 2-liter bottles, labels and caps removed
» Scissors
» Masking tape
» Permanent marker
» Four tall clear plastic cups
» Three coffee filters
» Three rubber bands
» Styrofoam packing peanuts
» Sand
» Pebbles
» Clock or stopwatch
» Adult supervisor

Steps to Success:

1. Put on the gardening gloves. Put two or three handfuls of potting soil into the first empty 2-liter bottle. Add water to fill the bottle about halfway and screw on the cap. Shake well. The bottle now holds the dirty water you will try to clean.

2. Ask an adult to cut the three empty bottles about 5 inches (13 centimeters) from the top. Discard the bottoms.

ADULT SUPERVISION REQUIRED

3. Label the three bottles Filter 1, Filter 2, and Filter 3. Do the same for three of the plastic cups.

Continued ⊖

4. Place a coffee filter over the narrow end of each bottle (the end you would normally pour from) and secure it tightly with a rubber band. This will keep the filtering material from falling out.

5. Fill the bottle labeled Filter 1 with about 3 inches (8 centimeters) of Styrofoam pieces. Fill the Filter 2 bottle with an equal amount of sand and the Filter 3 bottle with the same amount of pebbles.

6. Shake the 2-liter bottle of dirty water again to make sure the water and soil are mixed. Fill the remaining plastic cup halfway with the dirty water.

7. Rest the Filter 1 bottle on top of the Filter 1 cup, so the covered end of the bottle is inside the cup. Pour the dirty water into the filter. Observe how the soil particles stick to the Styrofoam. Record how long it takes for the water to completely drain into the cup. Wait until after the water has drained into the cup to remove the filter.

8. Repeat steps 6 and 7 using the Filter 2 filter and cup, and then the Filter 3 filter and cup. Be sure to use the exact same amount of dirty water for each.

9. Compare the colors of the water in the three cups.

Step 4

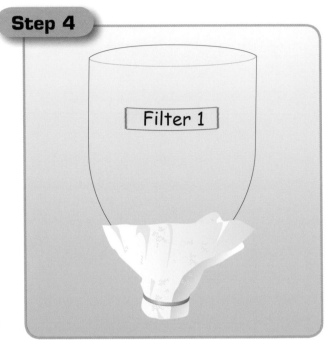

Step 7

Result Summary:

» Which filter worked best?

» Which worked worst?

» Which filter did it take the dirty water longest to filter through?

Added Activities to Give Your Project Extra Punch:

» Research how pollution from people and factories affects the natural filtration process.

» Create a single filter with even layers of each material. After the dirty water drains through the filter, take it apart and try to determine which layer did most of the "cleaning."

» Expand the project to test how well other materials, such as cotton balls, filter dirty water.

Display Extras:

» Include "before" and "after" photos or drawings of each filtering material. Also include photos or drawings of the dirty water before and after it passed through each filter.

» Re-create the setup of your three filters as part of your display.

The Disappearing Apple

When a tree dies in the forest, where does it go? Over time, it begins to disappear. We can thank **decomposers** for this. Decomposers, such as worms, termites, fungi, and microorganisms, feed on dead plant and animal matter. This matter eventually becomes part of the soil. How much do decomposers affect an ecosystem? In this experiment, you'll compare how quickly apples decompose with and without an added decomposer.

Do Your Research

Before you start, find out more about decomposers and the role they play in an ecosystem. Also research the fungus yeast, which you'll use as a decomposer in this experiment. After you have done your research, you will be ready to do the experiment or one similar to it. During this experiment, be sure to keep the sealed bags out of the reach of small children. The bags should be clearly marked as part of your experiment. Eating rotten apples covered in yeast is dangerous and can make people very sick!

Project Information

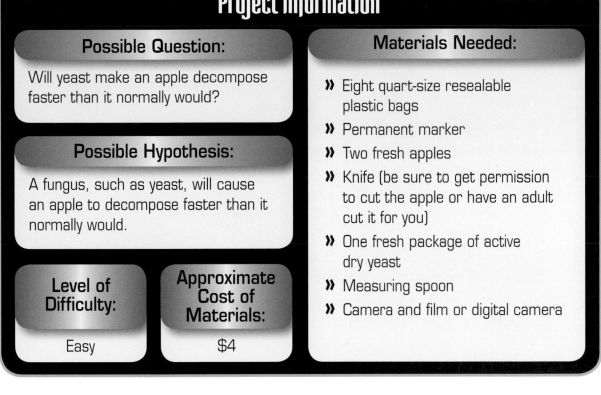

Possible Question:

Will yeast make an apple decompose faster than it normally would?

Possible Hypothesis:

A fungus, such as yeast, will cause an apple to decompose faster than it normally would.

Level of Difficulty:

Easy

Approximate Cost of Materials:

$4

Materials Needed:

» Eight quart-size resealable plastic bags
» Permanent marker
» Two fresh apples
» Knife (be sure to get permission to cut the apple or have an adult cut it for you)
» One fresh package of active dry yeast
» Measuring spoon
» Camera and film or digital camera

Here are some books and websites you could start with in your research:

» Lappi, Megan. *Decomposers*. New York: Weigl Publishers, 2004.
» Spilsbury, Richard and Louise. *Food Chains and Webs: From Producers to Decomposers*. Chicago: Heinemann, 2004.
» What Is a Decomposer?
http://www.qrg.northwestern.edu/projects/marssim/simhtml/info/whats-a-decomposer.html
» Recycle Works Kids: Decomposers
http://www.recycleworks.org/kids/decomposers.html

Steps to Success:

1. Label four of the plastic bags Yeast and the other four No Yeast.
2. Cut the apples into four equal pieces.
3. Place one apple slice in each bag.

Continued →

4. Measure 1 teaspoon (5 grams) of yeast. Pour the yeast onto the white part of the apple slices in the four Yeast bags. Seal the bags.

5. Without adding any yeast, seal the No Yeast bags.

6. Take photos of each bag. Be sure to keep the bags out of the reach of small children and pets.

7. Observe the apples each day. In your research journal, note any changes you see. Take photos or make drawings of each apple every two days.

8. Continue to observe the apples for at least one week. Compare how quickly the apples in the bags decompose.

9. When you complete the experiment, throw the sealed bags with the apples in them into the garbage.

Step 8

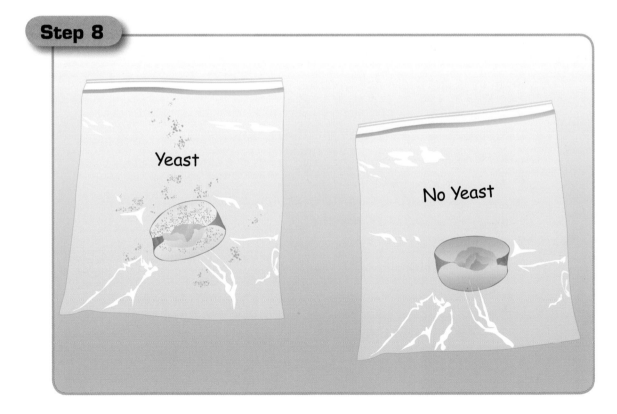

Result Summary:

» Which apples decomposed the fastest?
» What types of changes occurred?

Added Activities to Give Your Project Extra Punch:

» Vary the amount of yeast on additional apple slices and compare the results to those in the original project.

» Test whether different types of apples decompose faster than others. Or test whether apples of the same type decompose faster if one is ripe and one is not.

» Do the experiment with foods other than apples, such as bananas or potatoes, and compare the results.

Display Extras:

» Include the photos you took of each of the apple slices during the experiment.

» Attach pictures of decomposers, such as mushrooms growing on a rotted log or vultures flying over a carcass.

The apples in this bushel decomposed at different rates. What factors might have been involved?

Puddle and Pond pH

Ecosystems are made up of different sources of water—some contain salt and some are fresh water. One other key difference is the **acidity** of different bodies of water. The acidity of the water source affects all life that uses the water. In this experiment, you will compare the **pH** of different bodies of water in your hometown, such as tap water, rainwater, ponds, puddles, and lakes.

Do Your Research

In this project, you'll test the acidity of different water sources using pH paper. Make sure you choose safe bodies of water to test; wear gloves if necessary. Avoid putting yourself in a dangerous position as you collect water samples. Have an adult accompany you to gather samples from sources in nature, such as ponds or lakes. It's best to start this project before a rainstorm so you can later collect and test rainwater and puddles. Find out more about the pH scale and how pH paper works. Also learn more about acids and bases. Afterward, you'll be ready to try this experiment, or you may want to create your own.

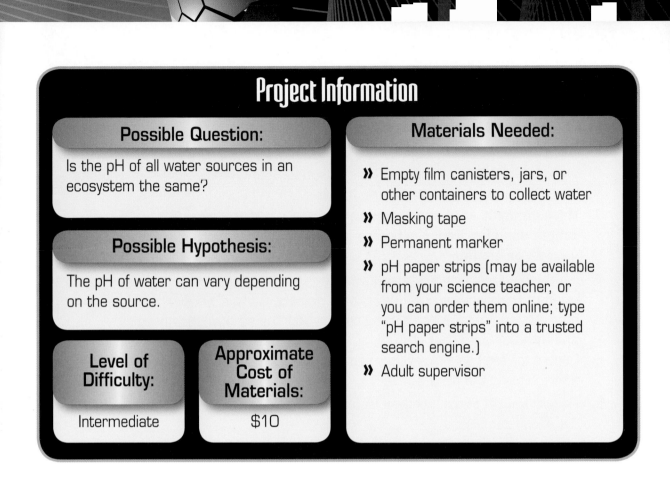

Project Information

Possible Question:

Is the pH of all water sources in an ecosystem the same?

Possible Hypothesis:

The pH of water can vary depending on the source.

Level of Difficulty:

Intermediate

Approximate Cost of Materials:

$10

Materials Needed:

» Empty film canisters, jars, or other containers to collect water
» Masking tape
» Permanent marker
» pH paper strips (may be available from your science teacher, or you can order them online; type "pH paper strips" into a trusted search engine.)
» Adult supervisor

Here are some books and websites you could start with in your research:

» Baldwin, Carol. *Material Matters: Acids and Bases.* Chicago: Raintree, 2004.
» Ballard, Carol. *How We Use Water.* Chicago: Raintree, 2005.
» Gallant, Roy A. *Water: Our Precious Resource.* New York: Benchmark, 2003.
» Kids' Corner: pH Scale
http://www.ec.gc.ca/acidrain/kids.html
» Water Quality Testing: pH Levels
http://www.bpa.gov/corporate/kr/ed/kidsinthecreek/topics/waterquality/ph.htm

Continued ⊕

Steps to Success:

1. Fill one container with tap water. Label the container.

2. Decide what bodies of water you are going to test, such as a lake, a puddle, and a pond. Label the containers with the names of the water sources you will test. Use at least one container to collect rainwater.

3. **Have an adult accompany you as you collect samples from the bodies of water you will be testing.**

ADULT
SUPERVISION
REQUIRED

4. Follow the directions on the container for using the pH paper strips. They should instruct you to dip one end of a strip into one of your water samples. Wait for the strip to change color, and then compare your strip to the color key provided with the paper. Repeat for the remaining water samples. Be sure to wash your hands after handling the pH paper.

5. Record the pH of each body of water in a chart. Compare the pH levels of the water samples.

Step 4

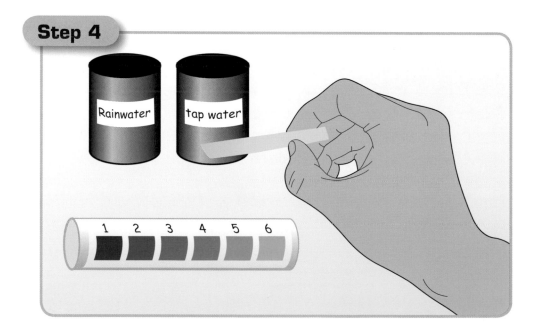

Result Summary:

» Which water sample was the most acidic (closest to 0)?
» Were any samples **alkaline**—above 7 on the pH scale?
» Which two bodies of water were the closest in pH?
» What factors may have had an effect on the pH of certain samples, such as the one taken from a puddle?

Added Activities to Give Your Project Extra Punch:

» Compare the pH levels of rainwater taken from the same location on different days.
» Research the ways acid rain and pollution can affect the pH level of bodies of water and the organisms that live there.

Display Extras:

» Include photos of each body of water you tested.
» Use crayons or markers to create a chart that shows the colors your pH paper turned for each sample.

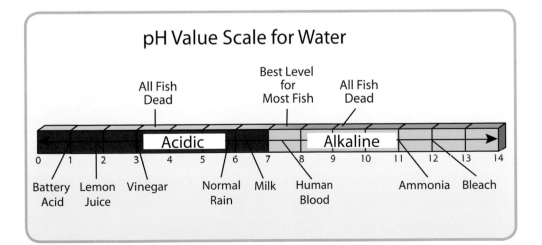

pH Value Scale for Water

No Good Water

In the previous project ("Puddle and Pond pH"), you learned about how the pH level is different in various water sources. Pollutants can change the pH level of rain to make it more acidic. Acid rain can cause damage to statues and buildings and can also destroy forests and plant life. In this experiment, you will test the effect that high levels of an acid have on plants.

Do Your Research

In this project, you will water plants with different combinations of vinegar. Because vinegar is an acid, be sure to wash your hands after doing the experiment. Before you begin, research the causes of acid rain and how it affects plants, animals, and even buildings and statues. You will also need a good understanding of the pH scale. After learning about acid rain and pH, you'll be ready to begin this project—or you may come up with your own.

Here are some books and websites you could start with in your research:

» Gallant, Roy A. *Water: Our Precious Resource*. New York: Benchmark, 2003.
» Kudlinski, Kathleen V. *How Plants Survive*. Philadelphia: Chelsea Clubhouse, 2003.
» EPA Acid Rain Students Site
   http://www.epa.gov/acidrain/site_students/index.html

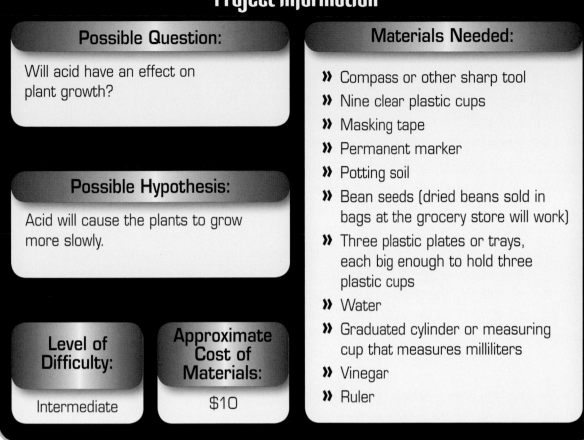

Project Information

Possible Question:

Will acid have an effect on plant growth?

Possible Hypothesis:

Acid will cause the plants to grow more slowly.

Level of Difficulty:

Intermediate

Approximate Cost of Materials:

$10

Materials Needed:

» Compass or other sharp tool
» Nine clear plastic cups
» Masking tape
» Permanent marker
» Potting soil
» Bean seeds (dried beans sold in bags at the grocery store will work)
» Three plastic plates or trays, each big enough to hold three plastic cups
» Water
» Graduated cylinder or measuring cup that measures milliliters
» Vinegar
» Ruler

» Young People's Trust for the Environment: Acid Rain
http://www.yptenc.org.uk/docs/factsheets/env_facts/acid_rain.html
» Kids' Corner: pH Scale: http://www.ec.gc.ca/acidrain/kids.html

Steps to Success:

1. Use the compass to carefully poke a few holes in the bottom of each cup. Label three cups Water 1, Water 2, and Water 3. Label three cups 50% Vinegar 1, 50% Vinegar 2, and 50% Vinegar 3. Label the last three cups 100% Vinegar 1, 100% Vinegar 2, and 100% Vinegar 3.

2. Fill each cup with soil to within about ½ inch (1.25 centimeters) of the top.

Continued ⟶

3. Poke your finger about ½ inch (1.25 centimeters) into the center of the soil. Place three seeds in each hole and cover with soil.

4. Place one group of cups on each tray. Place the trays by a window where all the cups will receive an equal amount of sunlight.

5. Water each cup just enough to moisten the soil, about 60 milliliters. Leave any water that drains through on the tray.

6. Observe the cups every other day. Record the day each seed germinates and measure and record each seed's growth in your research journal. If the soil is dry to the touch, add about 30 milliliters of water to each cup.

7. Once the plants are at least 1 inch (2.5 centimeters) tall—after about one week—water each cup with the appropriate liquid. Add 50 milliliters of water to the cups labeled Water. For the 50% Vinegar cups, mix 25 milliliters of vinegar with 25 milliliters of water and pour into the cups. Add 50 milliliters of vinegar to the cups labeled 100% Vinegar. Be sure to keep the vinegar out of the reach of small children and pets.

8. Continue to record the height of each plant in your research journal. Include a description of what the soil looks like each day and draw pictures of the plants as they change.

9. Continue to water the plants as needed (when the soil feels dry to the touch) with the same amount of the liquids from step 7.

10. Continue to record the growth of the plants for two more weeks. Compare the growth of the plants in the cups.

Step 7

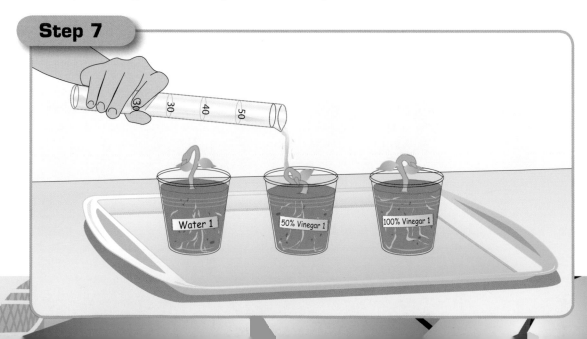

Result Summary:

» Which plant grew the tallest?
» What changes did you notice in the plants after you added the vinegar?
» Did you notice any changes to the soil?

Added Activities to Give Your Project Extra Punch:

» Repeat the experiment using other common natural acids, such as lemon juice and orange juice, and compare the results.
» Test plants that grow better in acidic soils, such as azaleas and rhododendrons, with ones that grow better in neutral soils. Repot the plants so they are all in the same type of soil.

Display Extras:

» Take a picture of the plants every other day and include the photos on your board.
» Create a line or bar graph of the plants' growth.

The Competition

Learning is its own reward, but winning the science fair is pretty fun, too. Here are some things to keep in mind if you want to do well in the competition:

1) Creativity counts. Do not simply copy an experiment from this or any other book. You need to change the experiment so that it is uniquely your own.

2) You will need to be able to explain your project to the judges. Being able to talk intelligently about your work will help reassure the judges that you learned something and that you did the work yourself. You may have to repeat the same information to different judges, so make sure you've practiced ahead of time. You will also need to be able to answer the judges' questions about your methods and results.

3) You will need to present your materials in an appealing manner. Discuss with your teacher whether or not it is acceptable to have someone help you with artistic flourishes to your display.

Keep these guidelines in mind for your display:

» **Type and print:** Display the project title, the question, the hypothesis, and the collected **data** in clean, neatly crafted paper printouts that you can mount on a sturdy poster display.

» **Visibility:** Be sure to print your title and headings in large type and in energetic colors. If your project is about the Sun, you might use bright reds, oranges, and yellows to bring your letters to life. If your project is about plant life, you might use greens and browns to capture an earthy mood. You want your project to be easily visible in a crowd of other projects.

» **Standing display:** Be sure your display can stand on its own. Office supply stores have thick single-, double-, and triple-section display boards available in several sizes and colors that will work nicely as the canvas for your science fair masterpiece. Mount your core data—your discoveries—on this display, along with photos and other relevant materials (charts, resource articles, interviews, etc.).

» **Attire:** Dress neatly and comfortably for the fair. You may be standing on your feet for a long time.

4) The final report is an important part of your project.
   Make sure the following things are in your final report:

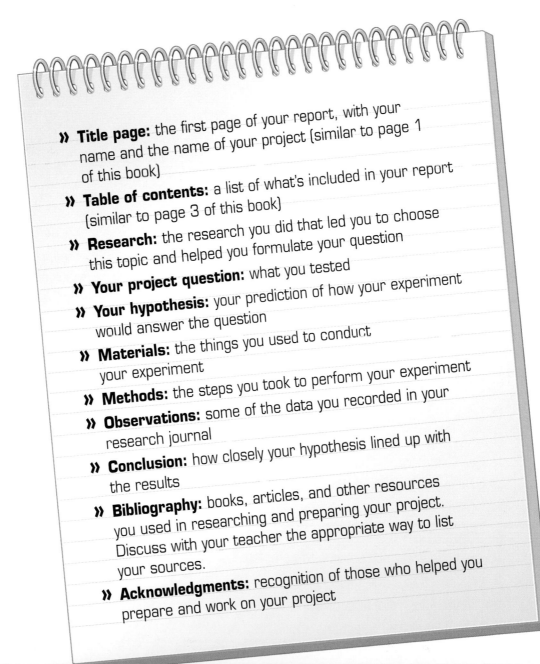

» **Title page:** the first page of your report, with your name and the name of your project (similar to page 1 of this book)

» **Table of contents:** a list of what's included in your report (similar to page 3 of this book)

» **Research:** the research you did that led you to choose this topic and helped you formulate your question

» **Your project question:** what you tested

» **Your hypothesis:** your prediction of how your experiment would answer the question

» **Materials:** the things you used to conduct your experiment

» **Methods:** the steps you took to perform your experiment

» **Observations:** some of the data you recorded in your research journal

» **Conclusion:** how closely your hypothesis lined up with the results

» **Bibliography:** books, articles, and other resources you used in researching and preparing your project. Discuss with your teacher the appropriate way to list your sources.

» **Acknowledgments:** recognition of those who helped you prepare and work on your project

Prepare to Be Judged

Each science fair is different, but you will probably be assigned points based on your performance in each of the categories below. Make sure to talk to your teacher about how your specific science fair will be judged. Ask yourself the questions in each category to see whether you've done the best possible job.

Your objectives

» Did you present original, creative ideas?

» Did you state the problem or question clearly?

» Did you define the variables and use controls?

» Did you relate your research to the problem or question?

Your skills

» Do you understand your results?

» Did you do your own work? It's OK for an adult to help you for safety reasons, but not to do the work for you. If you cannot explain the experiment, the equipment, and the steps you took, the judges may not believe that you did your own work.

Data collection and interpretation

» Did you keep a research journal?

» Was your experiment planned correctly to collect the data you needed?

» Did you correctly interpret your results?

» Could someone else repeat the experiment by reading your report?

» Are your conclusions based only on the results of your experiment?

Presentation

» Is your display attractive and complete?

» Do you have a complete report?

» Did you use reliable sources and document them correctly?

» Can you answer questions about your work?

Glossary

abiotic nonliving

acidity amount of acid in a substance. An acid is a compound with a pH below 7.

alkaline describes a compound with a pH above 7

allelopathic able to release chemicals that kill surrounding plants

atmosphere layer of gases that surrounds Earth

biotic living

carnivore animal that eats meat

carrying capacity maximum number of a given species that an area can support

control sample in an experiment that is left unchanged and used for comparison with other samples that have variables

data factual information

decomposer organism that breaks down dead plants or animals

food chain system in which energy is passed from plants to animals

germinate begin to grow; sprout

greenhouse effect warming of Earth's surface caused by heat and moisture trapped by the atmosphere

groundwater underground water that feeds wells and springs

herbivore animal that eats plants

hypothesis informed guess based on information at hand

invasives plants or animals that are not native to an area

pH measure of whether a substance is an acid or a base

producer organism that can make its own food

prediction say in advance what you think will happen, based on scientific study

quadrat survey scientific study in which conditions within two or more equal-size sample sections of a larger area are compared

regurgitate discharge food from the stomach through the mouth

scientific theory belief based on tested evidence and facts

variable something that can change; is not set or fixed

water cycle continuous cycle in which water moves from Earth to the atmosphere and back again

Index